# of Songs

EROTIC LOVE POETRY

WILLIAM B. EERDMANS PUBLISHING COMPANY

Grand Rapids, Michigan / Cambridge, U.K.

Published by
WM. B. EERDMANS PUBLISHING CO.
255 Jefferson Ave. S.E., Grand Rapids, Michigan 49503 /
P.O. Box 163, Cambridge CB3 9PU U.K.
www.eerdmans.com

Manufactured in China

07 06 05 04 03   7 6 5 4 3 2 1

Library of Congress Cataloging-in-Publication Data

Ernst, Judith.
Song of songs : erotic love poetry / adapted and illustrated by Judith Ernst.
p.   cm.
ISBN 0-8028-3990-8
1. Bible. O.T. Song of Solomon – Criticism, interpretation, etc.   2. Erotic poetry.
I. Ernst, Judith.   II. Title.

BS1485.52 .E76 2003
223′.9077 – dc21

2002029492

CONTENTS

Acknowledgments

Anumber of people have helped me during the course of this project. Thanks to Susie Schopler for the use of her photos, as well as for her intelligent support; and to Rosie Renkow for her color suggestions and her unflagging interest in the paintings, and for bringing her friends around to check on them as they progressed; to Phyllis Tickle for her enthusiasm and sensitive understanding of the project, and to Sheila Pinkel for her incisive comments and networking ideas; and to Cheryl Exum for her scholarship and interest in this project. Thanks also to Joyce Kachergis, Anne Theilgard, John August Swanson, Nancy Cheng, Michael Ernst, Rkia Cornell, John Bussanich, photographer John Rosenthal, and to my lawyer, Daniel Abraham.

I would especially like to thank my editor, Sandra De Groot, for her resolute support of this project and for her vision in helping to shape it; and David James Duncan for his fearless intuition and exemplary friendship, as well as for his remarkable introduction.

I am deeply indebted to Prof. Jack Sasson of Vanderbilt University for his generosity in comparing the English text with the original Hebrew. Any elegant phrases that readers find substantially different from those in the King James Bible are most likely a result of his kind efforts.

My heartfelt gratitude goes to my two daughters, Sophie and Tess, for their enthusiastic and loving support of their mom. Thanks also for the excellent modeling skills, Sophie, and the astute visual comments, Tess. Finally, I wish to dedicate this book to my husband, Carl Ernst, for first introducing me to the Song of Songs and for keeping that longing alive.

"I Will Climb the Palm Tree . . .":
A Song of Songs Introduction
in Two Parts

1

If anything is sacred, the human body is sacred.

— Walt Whitman

The Song of Songs is so unlike every other book of the Bible that it seems, at a glance, like a lost chapter from a different volume. Most of its verses are spoken by an imaginative and impassioned woman — the only such voice heard in the Bible. God is not mentioned once. Solomon passes in the distance but makes no dramatic appearance, and the male and female heroes remain anonymous. No history is set down, no prophecies, rules, or preachments are given. No theological points are made. But strangest of all is the topic. A few samples:

Her: *Let him kiss me with the kisses of his mouth . . . I sleep, but my heart wakes: It is the voice of my beloved, saying,*

"Open to me, my sister, my love, my dove, my pure one . . ." I have removed my robe . . . I have bathed my feet . . . I am sick with love . . . He shall lie all night betwixt my breasts . . .

Him: *This form of yours is like a palm tree . . . I will climb the palm tree, I will take hold of the boughs. May your breasts be as clusters of the vine, your breath as the scent of apples, and your mouth as the choicest wine going down sweetly, my beloved, trickling over the lips of sleepers . . .*

The subject of this book is erotic passion as expressed, alternatingly, by a woman or a man madly in love. The result is an underlying intensity of voice and purpose that Socrates once called "the erotic mania of the soul for the divine." The mania is inspired by the physical forms of a beautiful woman and an equally beautiful man. The mood is more that of a Hebrew Whitman or Blake than a Moses. And the music of the Songs reminds me of certain bards of pre-Christian Europe — as when the Irish hero, Fionn MacCool, first sets eyes on his beloved and cries: "Love makes us poor! We have not eyes enough to see all that is to be seen, nor hands enough to seize the tenth of all we want. When I look in her eyes I am tormented because I am not looking at her lips. When I look at her lips my soul cries, 'Her eyes! Look at her eyes!' "

Yet the book containing these verses is the Bible! Readers unamazed by this have, I dare say, not read much Christian history. The survival of these openly erotic and mystical songs in the same text touted by generations of Puritans, Conquistadors, Inquisitors, misogynist priests, and fundamentalist book burners is an outright miracle of fidelity to holy writ.

The contrast in content between the Songs and the rest of the Old Testament underlines this miracle: in Genesis we have Adam and Eve cast out of Eden almost the instant they awaken in it, then humanity cursed by God forever, Cain's murder of Abel, a second curse placed on humanity forever, then every man, woman, and child on earth but Noah's family drowned for "iniquity"; we have book after book of plagues, spies, rebellions, punishments, enslavements, exiles, and pained wanderings; we have long lists of (doomed) generations, followed by lists of rules and duties, followed by more lists of "perverse and crooked generations" to compare, always damnably, to Jehovah's prickly perfectionism, then "smite, hip and thigh, with a great slaughter." By the time the Ecclesiastes poet groans, "Vanity, vanity, all is vanity" we nearly feel bludgeoned into agreement.

Then comes the Song of Songs — and where O where have we landed? Lips suddenly made for kissing! The loveliest of bodies made not to smite but to adore and ravish. Breasts created not that thrice-cursed infants might suck a little pap before doomsday, but that a lover might caress and coddle then pillow his head between them. The beloved's body not a thing to deny as temptation, but a sacred gift to be lured, ASAP, into the most intimate possible contact with our own body. Sexual union openly pined for! Defiance of authority! Sleepless hearts! Midnight and midday trysts! Who wrote these verses? Physical and spiritual yearning are here so fiercely mingled that they fuse, creating a world within the world with its own holy laws.

2

Love means abandoning the people of the attributes
while forging intimacy with the people of the essence.

— Ruzbihan Baqli

The Song of Songs is beloved by the mystics. Indeed, John of the Cross, Teresa of Avila, Bernard of Clairvaux, Richard Rolle, the great French "Quietist" Madame Guyon, and others have written glowingly of it, and Rabbi Akiva declared the Songs nothing less than "the Holy of Holies." For non-mystical theologians, however, these verses have proven well-nigh impossible to interpret, for their purpose is blissfully a-theological.

Mainstream dogmatic theology for the most part denies or distrusts the body and stresses an infinite gulf between God and humans, citing "the Fall" as the cause of mortality and "original sin" as the reason for our Maker's judgments and punishment of our kind. The mystics, on the other hand, stress not the gulf but the astonishing intimacy between humans and God. Naming each of us "brides" or "lovers," God "the Beloved," and Christ "the Groom," they perceive love in all its forms as an eternal interplay between lover and Beloved and openly yearn, like the Song of Songs' poet, for union with Love Itself.

Mystical yearning, in the Song of Songs, is played out in vividly physical bodies, yet for all their beauty these bodies are not just mortal objects: they are essences of a holy homeland and gorgeous gifts and mysteries of God. In the imagery of the verses, God's art, the divine art, is the creation, and the essence of that art is the body of the beloved. The beloved's form and incomparably desirable parts are described in surprisingly specific botanical, biological, and geographical imagery. The love with which this imagery is infused radiates two ways. When the eyes of the beloved are compared to "pools in Heshbon, by the gate of Bathrabbim," when legs are likened to cedars of Lebanon, when the head is "Mount Carmel," the breasts "fawns" or "fruits," the lips "honeycomb," the well beneath the tongue "milk and honey," and the breath "apples," we feel not just the bliss of lovers lost in one another but the love of an entire people come home, after long, harsh exile, to their promised and holy land.

The result is a spirituality of Yes! and More Yes! Insofar as the body houses the soul it is holy — and insofar as the body is comprised of all that we eat it is doubly holy, for it is literally *of* the land, it is the essence of the land. This doubled intensity of feeling creates what we might call an eroticism of loving sacrifice. In taking the beloved in love, one consumes her. In offering oneself to the beloved, one is consumed. Yet what one is offering, receiving, and celebrating here is not just one person and the sexual act, but the herds of the holy hills, the figs, fruits, and spices, the orchards, honeycomb, milk, secret gardens, and wells of living waters so emphatically seen, in these verses, as components of the body. The beloved's body is not just likened to these divine gifts: the gifts can be literally touched, felt, and tasted in her body. Through each other, lovers literally drink, eat, and know the holy gift that is the land.

Where is the line between such lovemaking and worship? When the Everything-that-has-made-my-Beloved is precisely what and whom we yearn for and make love to — when this same "Everything" is what we offer her in return — Who is making love to Whom? To seek and cherish our beloved, as the Song of Songs has it, is to seek and cherish, via our bodies, the art and Artist that give us bodies. The "double beloved" lets us feel this. She/He is the spiritual lodestone. This is her quintessential beauty, and the undying beauty of these poems.

David James Duncan
Lolo, Montana
May 2002

Song of Songs

Song

The Song of Songs,
which is Solomon's —

Let him kiss me with the kisses of his mouth — for your love is better than wine. Because of the sweet fragrance of your ointment your name is as ointment poured forth. Therefore do the maidens love you. Draw me, and we will run quickly after you. The king has brought me into his chambers. We will be glad and rejoice in you, we will remember your love more than wine; sincerely do they all love you.

I am dark and beautiful, O daughters of Jerusalem,
as the tents of Kedar, as the curtains of Solomon.

I am dark and beautiful, O daughters of Jerusalem,
as the tents of Kedar, as the curtains of Solomon.
Stare not at me because I am dark, because the sun
has scorched me. My mother's children were angry
with me. They made me a keeper of vineyards; but
my own vineyard I have not kept. Tell me, you whom
my soul loves, where you feed, where you rest your
flock at noon, for why should I be as one lost among
the flocks of your companions? If you know not, O
fairest of women, follow the footsteps of the flock,
and feed your goats beside the shepherds' tents. ❋
I compare you, my love, to a mare among the chariots
of Pharaoh. Your cheeks are comely with rows of

jewels, your neck with chains of gold. We will make you borders of gold with studs of silver. While the king sits at his table, my spikenard releases its fragrance. As a bundle of myrrh is my well beloved to me; he shall lie all night between my breasts. My beloved is to me a cluster of henna in the vineyards of Engedi. Behold, you are fair, my love! Behold, you are fair, with eyes shapely as doves. You are truly fair, my beloved, yes pleasant. Our bed is indeed luxuriant, the beams of our house are cedar, and our rafters are fir.

I am dark and beautiful —

From the very beginning of the Song of Songs, its language is seductive and intimate, conveying to the reader an intoxicating experience, a sensuous desire. We know immediately that this is something unexpected from the Bible. The woman expresses emphatically, without hesitation or shame, her desire for the erotic attentions of her lover. But in spite of her ardent declaration, there is a shift of pronoun, adding a subtle ambiguity to the point of view expressed. Having started with "Let *him* kiss me with the kisses of *his* mouth . . . ," it ends with ". . . for *your* love is better than wine." At first we suppose that the woman is alone, wishing for her lover's kisses, but then it seems that she addresses him directly, either in his presence or in her imagination. This sliding perspective is one of the more extreme examples of the ease with which the voices change throughout the Song of Songs. Is the woman speaking to her lover as we listen? Is she describing his beauty, or is he extolling her charms? Perhaps she remembers how he spoke to her in an intimate moment, or what she whispered to him. We wonder if she imagines a colloquy in which she expresses her love for him, or he declares his passion for her. Is her lover King Solomon himself, or perhaps just a shepherd or some other anonymous but beautiful young man whom she loves? It is tempting to try to pin down the voices, or to try to put together a cogent narrative, making the poem more concrete and rationally understandable. If we surrender ourselves to the ambiguity described above, however, we allow a creative fluidity from which the Song of Songs can speak much more fully, more impressionistically, more lyrically.

There is the suggestion here that the "dark and beautiful" woman who speaks has been cast out from her family, made to work in the sun-baked vineyards, perhaps because she has been less than chaste and has not kept her "own vineyard." She wants to see her lover, whose soul she loves; he directs her to meet him beside the shepherds' tents.

The two lovers each describe their sensuous attraction to the other. She attracts him with the power of a mare moving among the stallions that pull Pharaoh's chariots. His presence to her is like a balm of fragrant myrrh between her breasts.

Arise, my love, my fair one, and come away.

I am the rose of Sharon, a lily of the valleys. As the lily among thorns, so is my love among the daughters. As an apple tree among the trees of the wood, so is my beloved among the sons. I sat down under his shadow, and his fruit was sweet to my taste. He brought me to the banqueting hall, his love over me like a banner. Stay me with flagons, comfort me with apples, for I am sick with love. His left arm is beneath my head, his right arm embraces me. I charge you, O daughters of Jerusalem, by the roes and by the hinds of the field, that you stir not up, nor awaken love, 'til it please. ※ The voice of my beloved! Behold, he comes leaping over mountains, skipping over hills.

Like a roe or a young hart is my beloved, as he stands behind our wall and peers from the windows, showing himself through the lattice. My beloved spoke, and said to me, "Rise up, my love, my fair one, and come away. For the winter is past, the rain is over and gone. Flowers appear on the earth, the warbling of birds has begun, and the cooing of doves is heard in our land. The fig tree puts forth its green fruit, and the vines with budding grapes release their fragrance. Arise, my love, my fair one, and come away." ❊ O my dove, who hides in the clefts of rocks, in the recesses of the terrace, let me see you, let me hear your voice; for sweet is your voice, and comely is your form. Catch

us foxes, little foxes, spoilers of vines, for our vines
have tender grapes. My beloved is mine, and I am his.
He feeds among the lilies. Until the day breaks and
the shadows flee, turn, my beloved, and be like a roe
or a young hart upon the
mountains of Bether.

My beloved spoke —

Once again the woman declares her beauty and her uniqueness, likening herself to both a rose and a lily of the valley. She also praises the beauty of her lover, comparing him to an apple tree among the trees of the forest. Then she describes her breathless encounter with him in the banqueting hall. Her experience there is overpoweringly sweet and evocative of young love; we imagine her almost swooning in its intensity. The description is exquisitely personal, but it also assumes a public aspect when she refers to his love over her "like a banner." As the Song of Songs progresses, we will see repeated again and again this dynamic between the intimately personal and the public, the place of the individual's desires within the context of the community and its expectations.

The interlude in the banqueting hall is followed by the admonition that will be repeated three times in the course of the Song of Songs: please do not stir up these passions until it is time to consummate them. This buildup, starting with the breathless banquet scene and followed by her admonition, sets up the tension for the encounter that is about to happen. While in her family's home, she hears her lover from behind the lattice, imploring her to come away with him.

The lover who calls his beloved from behind the lattice to "come away" is not a suitor publicly sanctioned by her family, or at least not yet. Though later in the song the woman is sometimes referred to as a bride, it is important to keep in mind that the song is not for the most part about morality or society's conventions, though it does not ignore those imperatives. The song is about love and longing, which is most powerfully conveyed through descriptions of the separations, tribulations, and intense desire associated with young lovers.

While the song's images are sensual, even erotic, they should not be confused with modern media-driven notions of sexuality, which commodify the body and reduce sexuality to voyeurism. Instead, the song embraces longing fully — emotionally, spiritually, as well as physically — in a way that highlights the independent volition of two people who love and desire one another.

When we hear her lover's request that she come away with him, we don't know how she ultimately responds. We're sure that she wants to see his handsome form and hear his sweet voice. Does she want him to stay with her until the day breaks and shadows flee, and to spend that time behaving like an exuberant roe or a young hart? Or instead, does she wistfully ask him to turn away until day has come again, to wander longingly through the night like a young deer upon the lonely mountains of Bether?

I held him and would not let him go,
until I brought him into my mother's house . . .

Night after night on my bed I seek him, whom my soul loves. I seek him, but I find him not. I must rise now, and go about the city, in streets, and in broad ways, seeking him whom my soul loves. I sought him, but I found him not. The watchmen that go about the city found me and I said, "Did you see him, whom my soul loves?" No sooner did I pass them, than I found him, whom my soul loves. I held him and would not let him go, until I brought him into my mother's house, into the chamber of her that conceived me. ✳ I charge you, O daughters of Jerusalem, by the roes, and by the hinds of the field, that you stir not up, nor awaken love, 'til it please.

I seek him, whom my soul loves —

The woman confesses that every night, while in bed, in her imagination she desires the presence of her lover beside her. In a move that would be bold in any society, she goes out alone into the night, into the streets, seeking the one she loves. She looks and looks, but cannot find him. She asks the watchmen if they have seen him, and then quickly she finds him. Without an apparent thought for convention, the woman brings her lover into the intimate space of her family home, into her mother's house, "into the chamber of her that conceived me."

Once again, we hear the refrain admonishing the daughters of Jerusalem not to stir up her desire until the appropriate time. But why would this woman make this request, since the action has just described her inviting her lover into her mother's house in the middle of the night? One would think that invitation clearly implies impending lovemaking. This repeated refrain sometimes seems to exist outside of the action, almost as a chorus. Since voices change constantly in the Song of Songs, perhaps we are to assume that the speaker of this particular admonition is someone listening to the tale of the woman bringing her lover into her mother's house. Maybe the listener hears this story and responds by saying something like, "Ladies, please, tell me no more, or I might lose control."

Who is this rising out of the wilderness . . . ?

Who is this rising out of the wilderness like pillars of smoke, perfumed with myrrh and frankincense, with all the powdered spices of merchants? Behold, it is the litter of Solomon, with sixty warriors about it, Israel's most valiant. They bear swords and are practiced in war; each man holds his sword at his thigh, for fear of the night. King Solomon made himself a palanquin out of the wood of Lebanon. He made the pillars of silver, the bottom of gold, the covering of purple, and the interior was lovingly inlaid by the women of Jerusalem. Go forth, O women of Zion, and gaze at King Solomon, wearing the crown given him by his mother on his wedding day, on the day of the gladness of his heart.

Go forth, O women of Zion —

What is this apparition coming out of the forest, wafting the fragrance of myrrh and frankincense and the exotic spices of the East? We are told that it is the wedding procession of King Solomon, who wears the crown given to him by his mother on his wedding day, on the day of his greatest joy. The women of Zion are instructed to go out and watch the procession. But are we to understand that they actually see the wedding procession of King Solomon himself, or is the marriage of Solomon and his bride a model to which they should aspire? In their maidenly fantasies, do they imagine themselves as the bride that Solomon comes to join? Or in their joy are they and their lovers like Solomon and his bride on their wedding day?

You have ravished my heart, my sister, my bride;
you have ravished my heart with one of your glances . . .

Behold, you are fair, my love. Truly, you are fair; behind your locks your eyes are shapely doves. Your hair is as a flock of goats streaming down from Mount Gilead. Your teeth are like a flock of sheep, evenly shorn, coming up from the wash; every one bore twins and none among them is barren. Your lips are like a thread of scarlet, and your speech is comely. Your temples are like a slice of pomegranate within your locks. Your neck is as the tower of David, built for an armory, with a thousand shields upon it, all shields of mighty men. Your breasts are like two young fawns, twins of a doe, that feed among the lilies. Until the day breaks, and shadows flee, I will get me to the mountain of myrrh, and to the hill of frankincense. You are all fair, my love; there is no blemish in you. ❀ Come with me from Lebanon, my bride, with me from Lebanon. Peer down from the crest of Amana, from the crest of Senir and Hermon, from the dens of lions, from mountains with leopards. You have ravished my heart, my sister, my bride; you have ravished my heart with one of your glances, with one chain of your necklace. How fair is your love, my sister, my bride! How much better is your love than wine, and the smell of your ointment than all spices! Your lips, my bride, drop as the honeycomb; honey and milk are under your tongue, and the scent of your garment is like the fragrance of Lebanon.

Truly, you are fair —

Now the woman's charms are described through the eyes of her lover. This is one of the sections in the Song of Songs that seems to lend itself to parody in the modern context because of its use of archaic similes comparing parts of her body to physical images from the ancient world. These particular visualizations may seem strange to us, since they no longer resonate with our experience. However, it is certainly not unusual for modern writers and others to use similar descriptive devices, especially when they are used to evoke the shape of the female body. We do not seem to mind at all, for example, when we encounter advertisements using the image of a wine bottle, or a sports car, to mirror the curves of the feminine form. In contrast, the images in the Song of Songs are especially charming since they are such particularly visual evocations of the natural world. Take, for example, "your eyes are shapely doves." If you recall the simple caricature of a dove used as a symbol for peace, its curved lines are like the shapely lines of a beautiful, feminine eye. "Your hair is as a flock of goats streaming down from Mount Gilead." Imagine seeing a huge flock of black goats running down a mountain. From a distance, the effect would be like a moving wave of black, with the fur of the animals reflecting the sunlight — quite a stunning image. "Your teeth are like a flock of sheep, evenly shorn, coming up from the wash; every one bore twins and none among them is barren." In other words, her teeth are clean, white, evenly spaced, and she has them all. "Your neck is as the tower of David, built for an armory, with a thousand shields upon it." This image is important, because it implies that she is proud; her head is held high, and we imagine her jewelry decorating her long neck. "Your breasts are like two young fawns, twins of a doe, that feed among the lilies." This image is especially sweet. Imagine two fawns feeding, their necks arched down. Something catches their attention, and their heads bob up. Seen in profile, the line of their necks, extending down to their upturned noses, is a perfect image for the upper line of the breast, dipping to the nipple.

These visual descriptions lead up to her lover's declaration that he will enjoy the delights of love until dawn; his lover is perfect. All of this is the prelude to one of the most seductively beautiful parts of the Song of Songs, in which he invites his bride to "Come with me from Lebanon. . . ."

A garden enclosed is my sister, my bride;
a spring shut up, a fountain sealed.

A garden enclosed is my sister, my bride; a spring shut up, a fountain sealed. Your plants are an orchard of pomegranates, with pleasant fruits; camphire, with spikenard, spikenard and saffron; calamus and cinnamon, with all trees of frankin= cense; myrrh and aloes, with all the best of spices; a garden fountain, a well of living waters, streaming from Lebanon. ❋ Awake, O north wind; and come, O south! Blow upon my garden, that its spicy fragrance flows out. Let my beloved come into his garden, to eat his pleasant fruits. ❋ I am come into my garden, my sister, my bride. I have plucked my myrrh with my spice; I have eaten my honeycomb with my honey; I have drunk my wine with my milk. Eat, O friends! Drink, yes, drink deeply, O beloved!

Let my beloved come into his garden —

Here we read that his sister, his bride is like a walled garden, a closed spring, a sealed fountain. She is beautiful but inaccessible. How are we to understand this image when the speaker, in an apparent reversal, goes on to compare his lover to delicious fruits and fragrant spices in the garden, and ends by describing her as a flowing fountain, a well of living water streaming from Lebanon? Perhaps his bride is a closed garden to all but him, for whom she is a flowing fountain. In fact, she implores the wind to blow upon her garden, so that its spicy fragrance flows out, enticing her lover to come in and enjoy the fruits there. And he docs. He has come into his garden, he has plucked, he has eaten, and he has drunk. So should we all.

. . . if you find my beloved, tell him that I am sick with love.

I sleep, but my heart wakes: it is the voice of my beloved, knocking, saying, "Open to me, my sister, my love, my dove, my pure one, for my head is drenched with dew, and my locks with the drops of the night." I have removed my robe; am I to put it on? I have bathed my feet; am I to soil them? My beloved let go of the door's latch and my body thrilled for him. I rose up to open to my beloved. My hands, covered with myrrh, and my fingers with sweet-smelling myrrh dripped upon the handles of the lock. I opened to my beloved, but my beloved had withdrawn and was gone. My soul had failed when he spoke. I sought him, but could not find him. I called him, but he gave me no answer. The watchmen that went about the city found me; they struck me, they wounded me. The guards of the city walls stripped the mantle off me. I charge you, O daughters of Jerusalem, if you find my beloved, tell him that I am sick with love. ❋ How is your beloved better than others, O fairest among women? How is your beloved better than others, that you so charge us? My beloved is radiant and ruddy, the foremost among ten thousand. His brow is like the finest gold, his locks are curly and black as the raven. His eyes are doves by the river, washed with milk and fitly set. His cheeks are as beds of spices, banks of perfumed flowers; his lips are like lilies, dripping flowing myrrh. His hands are as gold cylinders, studded with beryl; his belly a board of bright ivory, overlaid with sapphires. His legs are pillars of marble, set in sockets of fine gold. His form is as Lebanon, choice as the cedars. His mouth is most sweet. Yes, he is altogether lovely. This is my beloved, and this is my friend, O daughters of Jerusalem.

I sleep, but my heart wakes —

This is one of the richest, most interesting sections of the Song of Songs. Though she sleeps, her heart is awake; she can hear the voice of her beloved at the door as he knocks, asking her to open to him. She hesitates; she demurs — she is too cozily tucked in bed, having already taken off her robe, already washed her feet. When he stops knocking, in an erotically charged passage she realizes that she must open the door to him. But in her moment of hesitation, he has left. So out she goes into the city to find him. She looks everywhere, but to no avail. This time her search for him in the city turns into a nightmare. The watchmen find her and beat her, and take her shawl. She is at her wit's end, experiencing the moment of greatest desperation over separation from her lover. This time the plea she addresses to her friends takes on a tragic tone, that if they find her beloved they should tell him that she is sick with longing for him.

Love and longing are not the monopoly of any one tradition or religion but have been eloquently written about all over the world. This part of the Song of Songs suggests mystical interpretations familiar in spiritual literature of various types — Sufi,

Hindu, and Christian. I am asleep to the truth, or gnosis, but my heart wakes. Though I do not understand God, or mystical truth, nevertheless I feel an opening in my heart. Her hesitation after she hears her lover at the door implies the idea that one must not be asleep or hesitate when the beloved, or God, comes. One must be vigilant, waiting for the opportunity, because it may be gone in a flash. We see this sentiment echoed in Persian poetry:

> If you wish the beloved's presence,
> Don't be absent, Hafiz!
> When you meet the one that you desire,
> Leave the world and let it go.[1]

The desperation that she experiences when she can't find her lover as she looks for him in the streets points to that moment when the pain of separation from the beloved, or God, is at its greatest. It is the dark night of the soul of St. John of the Cross, the period before union with the divine beloved when God seems most distant. It is the moment in the Gita Govinda when Radha realizes that she's alone in the dark forest, surrounded by the blackness of night, and that perhaps Krishna has spurned her.

While this passage from the Song of Songs has a similarity to mystical interpretations of awakening the heart, hesitation, and separation, the next passage brings us right back down to earth. Her friends ask the woman, quite understandably given her powerful response to her lover's absence, how is he better than others, what's so great about him? Why does separation from this man put her in such a state?

The woman then proceeds to describe the physical beauty of her lover, using a most spectacular series of comparisons. She lists the attractions of his brow, his beautiful black hair, his cheeks, lips, hands, legs, even his belly, finally summing up by saying that his mouth is most sweet and he is altogether lovely. Then she dramatically declares to the daughters of Jerusalem that he is not only her beloved, but also her dear friend.

In these two short related passages, the reader traverses the broad spectrum from mystical allusion, to highly erotic evocations of desire, to descriptions of physical beauty, to a declaration of true friendship with one's lover.

Who is she that looks forth like the dawn, fair as the moon,
clear as the sun, and terrible as an army with banners?

Where is your beloved gone, O fairest among women?
Where has your beloved turned aside, that we may seek
him with you? My beloved is gone down into his garden,
to the beds of spices, to browse in the gardens, and to
gather lilies. I am my beloved's and my beloved is mine.
He feeds among the lilies. ❋ You are beautiful, O my
love, as Tirzah, comely as Jerusalem, terrible as an army
with banners. Turn away your eyes from me, for they
overcome me. Your hair is as a flock of ewes streaming
down from Gilead. Your teeth are as a flock of sheep,
evenly shorn, coming up from the wash; every one bore
twins and none among them is barren. As a slice of
pomegranate are your cheeks, seen through your veil.

There are sixty queens, and eighty concubines, and maidens without number. But unique is my dove, my perfect one; favorite of her mother, a delight to her that bore her. Maidens bless her when they see her; yes, even queens and concubines praise her. Who is she that looks forth like the dawn, fair as the moon, clear as the sun, and terrible as an army with banners? I went down into the walnut grove to see the budding by the stream, to see if the vines blossomed, the pomegranates bloomed. Before I was aware, I fancied I saw the chariots of Amminadib. Turn, turn, O Shulamite! Turn, turn around, that we may gaze upon you. But what will you see when you gaze upon the Shulamite but a dance of two armies?

Even queens and concubines praise her —

The mood in this part of the song is striking. Twice the woman is described as being terrible as an army with banners. Though it starts off fairly straightforwardly, saying once again that she is beautiful, this time her beauty is not merely attractive but awe-inspiring. Her eyes overcome him with their power. The woman's physical attributes are enumerated, repeating some of the pastoral images seen earlier, but then the tone changes slightly, moving toward a more public assessment of his lover. She is unique, the favorite of her mother. Maidens bless her. She is compared to queens and concubines, who praise her.

This description is followed by a passage that is problematic for translators because of its cryptic references to the chariots of Amminadib and the Shulamite. No one really knows to what the "chariots of Amminadib" refer, nor do they quite know how to translate "Shulamite" or, in fact, the entire sentence, "But what will you see when you gaze upon the Shulamite but a dance of two armies?" Some translators have even omitted this part as untranslatable.

One way we may understand the term "Shulamite" is to associate it with war. In fact, in a recent commentary, Ariel and Channa Bloch note that one of the alternative translations of Shulamite is "a formal blend of the name of the Mesopotamian war goddess Shulmanitu (Ishtar) and 'Shunammite'" (one from the village of Shunem), though they do not use this interpretation in their translation.[2] The woman is compared to an army in her power to awe her lover; her eyes overcome him; queens praise her. Then her lover goes down into the walnut grove, and he imagines he sees a war-like apparition, the Shulamite, as well as the chariots, all reminding him of the glories of armies past, the nobility of his people. But what will this reaching for glories past really amount to but "a dance of two armies," or the maneuvering of battalions of soldiers? The stunning beauty of his beloved, and implicitly his love for her, far surpass in importance any vain notions of the glories of peoples, or of war.

Another interpretation that will resonate with modern readers is to understand the "dance of two armies" as referring to the so-called battle of the sexes, the push and pull experienced in male/female relationships caused by what we suppose is the inherent difference in perspective between the sexes. The speaker goes down into the walnut grove, has a war-like vision of the chariots of Amminadib, and then sees the Shulamite, who in this case is his beloved. Amid the allusions to her awe-inspiring presence, he realizes that there will be more to come in their relationship than just gardens, roses, and sensuality.

This form of yours is like a palm tree
and your breasts like clusters of grapes.

How beautiful are your feet in sandals, O prince's daughter! Your rounded thighs are like jewels, the handiwork of a cunning craftsman. Your navel is like a round goblet which never lacks wine. Your belly is like a heap of wheat circled by lilies. Your two breasts are like two fawns, twins of a gazelle. Your neck is as a tower of ivory; your eyes like pools in Heshbon, by the gate of Bathrabbim. Your nose is as a tower of Lebanon, which looks toward Damascus. The head upon you is like Carmel, and the locks on your head like purple; a king is caught in its tresses. How fair and how pleasant you are, O love, for delights! This form of yours is like a palm tree and your breasts like clusters of grapes. I said, "I will climb the palm tree, I will take hold of the boughs. May your breasts be as clusters of the vine, your breath as the scent of apples, and your mouth as the choicest wine going down sweetly, my beloved, trick= ling over the lips of sleepers."

'I will climb the palm tree —

Because of its overtly erotic nature, this is probably the most notorious section of the Song of Songs. Starting with her feet and going up, the woman's features are vividly described by her lover, comparing her various physical attributes to specific elements of the created world. Her rounded thighs are like jewels, her belly like a heap of wheat circled by lilies, her neck is a tower of ivory. The wording is especially seductive when it gets to the wonderfully musical effect of the ancient place names Heshbon and Bathrabbim. After lingering poetically over all of her various graces, her entire form is described by her lover as being like a palm tree and her breasts like clusters of grapes. He will climb the palm tree and take hold of the boughs. As he imagines this encounter, he expresses with a vivid set of images the fervent hope that he will savor completely all of her many charms.

Let us rise early for the vineyard; let us see if the vines flourish,
whether the tender grapes appear, the pomegranates bloom.
There will I give you my love.

I am my beloved's and his desire is for me. Come, my beloved, let us go forth into the field, let us lodge in the villages. Let us rise early for the vineyard; let us see if the vines flourish, whether the tender grapes appear, the pomegranates bloom. There will I give you my love. The mandrakes give a fragrance, and at our gates are all manner of choice fruits, new and old, that I have stored for you, beloved. O that you were my brother, that suckled at the breast of my mother! When I meet you in the streets I could kiss you and no one would despise me. I would pull and lead you to my mother's house, and you would teach me. I would have you drink spiced wine, of the juice of my pomegranates. His left arm should be under my head, and his right arm should embrace me. I charge you, O daughters of Jerusalem, that you stir not up, nor awaken love, 'til it please. Who is she that comes up from the wilderness, leaning upon her beloved? Under the apple tree I roused you; there did your mother conceive you, there did she who gave birth to you conceive you.

I am my beloved's —

I n this scene, a woman plans a rendezvous with her lover. They will go into the fields, into vineyards, staying in villages, and there she will give herself to him. In the biblical versions of the Song of Songs the line "O that you were my brother . . ." is the beginning of a new verse. However, run together with the preceding lines as in this version, it seems to reflect that though they meet in this idyllic spot, she would rather be meeting in a more comfortable, familiar location. Instead, they must hide their tryst. She wishes that they did not have to meet secretly, that they could show their affection for one another openly.

Once again, like in the banqueting scene, she expresses her apparent reverie that his left arm should be under her head, and his right arm should embrace her. This is followed by the now familiar admonition that the daughters of Jerusalem not stir up her desire until the time is ripe. The section ends by asking who the woman is who emerges from the wilderness leaning on her lover, and by referring to an arousal under an apple tree, the same spot where one of the lovers was conceived.

It is as if in the beginning lines of this passage we see the "before" shot, the woman planning an encounter with her lover. In the last lines, we see the couple after the consummation, after their tryst, coming out of the forest looking like lovers. In between this "before" and "after," once again the woman contemplates her love, her desire, and the difficulties inherent in dealing with these issues in the context of her community.

. . . for love is strong as death, jealousy is cruel as the grave.
Its darts are darts of fire, a flame forever blazing.

Set me as a seal upon your heart, as a seal upon your arm: for love is strong as death, jealousy is cruel as the grave. Its darts are darts of fire, a flame forever blazing. Many seas cannot quench love, nor can floods drown it. If a man gives all his household wealth for love, still he would be scorned. We have a little sister, so young she has no breasts. What shall we do for our sister once she is spoken for? If she be a wall, we will build upon her a palace of silver; and if she be a door, we will enclose her with boards of cedar. I am a wall, with breasts like towers, so I am favored in his eyes.

Set me as a seal upon your heart —

Many beautiful passages in the Song of Songs could be used in marriage ceremonies — for example, the passage that begins, "You have ravished my heart, my sister, my bride . . ."; or "A garden enclosed is my sister, my bride . . ." It is surprising, therefore, that the one passage that is most often quoted in marriages is this one. Perhaps it's quoted because it is one of the only places in the poem in which love is spoken of abstractly rather than with erotic specificity. In addition, the requested strong oath is suggestive of the promises spoken in a marriage ceremony.

Following this is one of the more peculiar passages in the song. It refers enigmatically to a sister still too young to have breasts. What will we do when our little sister starts to receive suitors? If she is a wall, or chaste, we will honor her, or "build upon her a palace of silver." But if she is a door, or promiscuous, we will, literally, bury her, or "enclose her with boards of cedar." This reiterates the seriousness of love, that it cannot be taken lightly. But since so many other parts of the poem imply less-than-sanctioned erotic encounters, this seemingly repressive position seems curious. However, we need not assume that the little sister's behavior is expected to be totally different than what we have seen before. Instead, perhaps promiscuity, or sex with many partners, is what is being objected to in this passage, rather than meeting with one's beloved. This is especially pertinent in conjunction with the beginning admonition to "Set me as a seal upon your heart . . ." and the following reference to jealousy. The passage ends with a woman declaring that she is a wall, her breasts like towers, so she's favored in her lover's eyes. Is she a wall to all but her lover, for whom she is a door? This understanding would mirror the imagery of the "garden enclosed," in which she is both a "fountain sealed" and a "well of living waters."

Make haste, my beloved, and be like a gazelle or a young hart
upon the mountains of spices.

Solomon had a vineyard at Baalhamon. He employed guards there, for everyone had to bring a thousand pieces of silver for its fruit. My vineyard is for me alone. You, O Solomon, keep your thousand, and the guardians of its fruit their two hundred! ✳ O woman who dwells in the garden, companions are listening to your voice; let me hear it. Make haste, my beloved, and be like a gazelle or a young hart upon the mountains of spices.

O woman who dwells in the garden —

Scholars have argued about the authorship of the Song of Songs. Was it written by one person, or by many? Is it a compilation of love songs, passed down through an oral tradition over a long period of time, which were strung together to make a whole? Or does it exhibit a coherence indicative of a single author? Was the poet (or poets) a woman, or a man? These questions have never really been answered, and continue, in fact, to be debated. Oftentimes authorship has been attributed to King Soloman, though he is only referred to in passing twice in the poem.

This last section of the Song of Songs begins with a passage about King Solomon's garden. It seems to be a boast that though Solomon is wealthy, his wealth itself determines that he must share his vineyard, whereas the speaker's vineyard is his alone. The speaker would not trade Solomon's wealth for his own good fortune, which is to possess entirely his own vineyard, which of course is also a metaphor for his lover. Vineyards and gardens being used interchangeably, this sets up the last two lines of the song. The male speaker calls to the woman who dwells in the garden, asking to hear her voice. She answers him as if he is her beloved, and once again, invites him to come to her and behave toward her like a young gazelle upon the "mountains of spices."

What are we to make of the Song of Songs which, in spite of its antiquity and its archaic images, still carries with it such charm and power, is still so touching to those who fall under its spell? The subject of love, even physical, erotic love, when it is conveyed with such beauty strikes a chord deep within us all. We have a profound longing to be whole, to be united with another, but this longing carries with it something more than just physical desire. The Sufi poet, Rumi, in the first part of his *Masnavi*, describes that longing as the plaintive song of the reed flute, lamenting its abrupt removal when it was cut from the reed bed, longing to be back again from where it came. It is the primordial longing of the created to be back, united with our origins, at one with the Creator. No one would deny that we are physical beings, that we are part of the created universe. Does not that physicality itself play an ineffable role in our spiritual journey? Many traditional stories from the Indian subcontinent, as well as the famous Persian story of Majnun and Leila, feature the motif of separated lovers who find a deeper spiritual longing and fulfillment through their intense yearning for one another.

As the great nineteenth-century South Asian poet, Ghalib, said, "From love, nature found the taste of life. It found the cure for pain — it found a pain with no cure."[3] In the continuum that includes both physical love, with all its emotional complexity, and that love and longing which is more sublime, it's hard to to know exactly where to draw lines or make distinctions. At its most poignant, human love and longing are touched by the fragrance of transcendence, of something beyond mere desire. Perhaps the twentieth-century mystic, Meher Baba, gave us a key to understanding the Song of Songs and love's importance when he said, "Love born in the Truth . . . is a pure blessing not only for yourself, but for each and all, for ever and ever, in the 'eternal now.'"[4]

END NOTES

[1] Hafiz, *Divan*, edited by Qasim Ghani and Muhammad Qazvini (Tehran: Amir Kabir, 1973), no. 1, p. 18, translated by Carl W. Ernst.

[2] Ariel and Channa Bloch, *The Song of Songs: A New Translation with an Introduction and Commentary* (New York: Random House, 1995), p. 197.

[3] Ghalib, *Divan-e Ghalib Musavvar, Naqsh-e Chughta'i* (Lahore: Ayvan-e Isha'at, n.d.), p. 5, translated by Carl W. Ernst.

[4] Meher Baba, *Life at Its Best*, edited by Ivy O. Duce (San Francisco: Sufism Reoriented, 1957), p. 58.

ARTIST'S NOTE

It was not until a few years ago that I actually sat down and read the Song of Songs. I recall hearing friends talk about it, referring to its beauty and eroticism, and in fact, my husband quoted it to me when we were courting. I was intrigued, with both him and the Song, but though I married him soon after, it was still many years before I read it.

I suppose I had trouble imagining love poetry in the context of the Old Testament. Like many people in my generation, I was not very familiar with the Old Testament, and I thought of it as being distant, authoritarian, and mostly about the patriarchs. What people often remember are fragments of oddly archaic stories, seemingly unconnected to an orienting source of understanding. Since most of us know very little about the history of Christianity or Judaism, nor especially about the more experiential mystical traditions associated with these religions, that lens through which one can view the Old Testament is often blocked. This is one of the reasons that so many people in the West in recent decades have looked to Asia for inspiration, seeking cultures that are still actively connected to the wellsprings of scripture, mysticism, oral history, and art.

In my case, I looked to India in the early 1970s, and over several trips I started to learn something about Indian religions, literature, and art. It was not surprising, then, that love poetry for me came to be epitomized by the *Gita Govinda*, the wonderful medieval Indian poem chronicling the love play between Radha and Krishna. The lovers experience all the delights of love, as well as its tribulations, but their interaction becomes more than just that of lovers. It becomes in the Indian context a personification of our underlying longing for union with God, the divine beloved, a longing that mystically drives all of creation. The Indian paintings that typically illustrate this poetry are exquisite, delicately capturing the sensuality of both Radha and Krishna. Yet the tone which is set by the breathtaking beauty of these paintings makes the spiritual content implicit to the viewer.

Another genre of Indian painting that influenced this Song of Songs is called *Barahmasa* ("twelve months"). These paintings accompany poems describing the yearning of a woman for her lover, who has gone away. Her mood of longing both reflects, and is reflected by, her physical environment, which changes with each of the twelve months in the Indian year. Imagine my surprise when I finally read the Song of Songs to discover how similar in mood, if not in content, it is to these Indian poetic and artistic genres. By deciding to paint the Song of Songs, I hoped to visually convey that sensuous mood of love and longing that at its highest reflects a touch of the divine.

The imagery for my paintings always starts in my imagination. The hard work comes in making the idea real in the material world, tangible as a work of art. That process, the work of bringing the imagined image out, is always creative and surprising, and provides its own kind of gratification. But it is different from the visualization, which is for me the truly creative aspect of the process, based on an essentially meditative experience. It is the formulation in the mind's eye of an ideal image.

In order to start visualizing the illustrations I had to first look closely at the text. The King James Bible is universally accepted as one of the most beautiful works ever written in English, so I wanted to stay as close as I could to that majestic and familiar language. But there are well-known problems with the King James version, not the least of which is the fact that it is written (as is much of the Old Testament) in an unrhymed verse form rather than as prose, or in paragraphs. The versification does nothing to enhance the language or the content of the Song of Songs. The text is broken by chapter and verse, oftentimes in a seemingly arbitrary fashion, and the length of lines within verses sometimes seems to be dictated by column width rather than poetic reason. For the modern reader, the accessibility of the King James Song of Songs is also hindered by archaic words, such as "thee," "thou," "cometh," and "goeth," which give it a formal, "from the Bible" tone, distancing it further from the reader. There are also some well-known obscurities in the King James version, like "The voice of the turtle is heard in the land," which should be understood as "The voice of the [turtle] dove . . ." I began to modify the text simply by rewriting the King James language as prose, taking it out of the verse form, modernizing the archaic usages mentioned above as I went along, and remedying the more well-known problematic words and phrases.

Furthermore, in order to illustrate the text, I had to select the places in it that most naturally lent themselves to my visualization. Having taken it out of verse form, I then broke it into selections that made visual as well as logical sense to me, using the visual to shape the poem and its interpretation. This was significant, since the resulting text, while not changing how the lines follow one another, nevertheless groups the traditionally numbered verses in ways that change the logical perspective of the reader, especially in certain passages.

The most important step came next, when I was able to show the amended text to Professor Jack Sasson, of the Department of Religious Studies at Vanderbilt University. He is not only a specialist in Hebrew and a great admirer of the Song of Songs, but also editor of the award-winning encyclopedia, *Civilizations of the Ancient Near East*. He kindly agreed to read the amended text, comparing it closely to the original Hebrew.

Professor Sasson's careful reading resulted in a number of suggestions for alternate phrasing, with his generous offer to "use whatever you like." In cases where I felt his suggestions clarified the Song, I readily adopted them; in cases where I felt either phrase could be used, I opted to go back to the familiarity of the King James version. The hybrid Song of Songs that resulted from this process is remarkably close in language to the King James Bible, but, at the same time, is strikingly different in its overall effect.

At this point in the work, the visualization process had started, and now I had to begin sketching the initial forms and compositions. While sometimes perspective is indicated in my paintings, it is always secondary to the two-dimensional composition. There is a reason for this. Our eyes see perspective. Though we can intellectually understand perspective as a phenomenon, it is a sensual experience rather than a contemplative one; it is how our eyes see distance. When a painting emphasizes visual perspective, the effect on the viewer is to direct the gaze into the distance, "out the back" of the painting, cutting short the intellectual dynamic between the viewer and the painting. Imagine what happens when the eye is not drawn to that vanishing point, instead being allowed to move around a two-dimensional graphic composition. This throws the sensual experience back to the mind of the viewer, setting up a dynamic relationship between the sensual and the contemplative. The painting can then become emblematic or mythic, something larger than just what is materially portrayed in the picture, something to be enjoyed intellectually by the viewer.

The next decision was about representation. Who should be portrayed in illustrations of the Song of Songs? Though both man and woman figure in the text, one of the most remarkable aspects of the Song of Songs is its overt, unashamed expression of a feminine sensuality, of a woman revealing her desire. Indeed, the entire Song seems to be expressed primarily in a feminine voice; some scholars have even suggested that it can be seen as one woman's monologue. This is especially striking in the context of the Old Testament, which we so associate with patriarchy and the male voice. Furthermore, in our culture it is especially rare to find feminine sensuality expressed visually, what we see, instead, are male expressions of what men find "sexy." I decided to focus my imagery entirely on the woman, or women, choosing to emphasize a restrained feminine sensibility that pictures longing for one's beloved rather than the implied fulfillment. I also wished to retain a quality of universality in the images. While suggesting ancient Palestine, the women should seem like they could be from any time or place. From a practical point of view, that universality would have been more difficult to portray with men, since there is more historical specificity in men's dress than there is in women's. Women from any time or place can be pictured wearing simple, long dresses, while men's clothing is much more determined by place, time, and function.

Details in the text suggested certain images as I was creating the illustrations. I tried to integrate plants and flowers appropriate to the geography of the biblical landscape, as well as to particular descriptions in the Song. The most dramatic example of this comes in the illustration on page 50, in which the woman is wandering the streets of the city, desperately in search of her beloved. The flowers pictured are capers, best known nowadays as an item found in the refrigerators of gourmet cooks. In ancient lore, however, capers symbolized desire. Even today, they grow in cracks of old buildings and walls in Jerusalem, opening their beautiful pink blossoms at night. I apologize to botanists, however, for taking some artistic license with the growing and blooming seasons.

My illustrations are a visual response to my creative reading of the Song of Songs. The paintings and my short commentary contain insights from my own experience — my travels, my reading of mystical literature from various times and cultures, and my exposure to art from around the world. The test of great literature is its ability to speak to different people from different times and places, allowing readers to find new, fresh ways in which the content enlightens them. This version of the Song of Songs is a response suited to a new era in which it is possible to focus on the feminine and move away from sectarian interpretations. It aims at preserving the Song's unusual and arresting flavor, retaining the archaic charm and mystery of the original while speaking to the hearts of modern readers with the dignified beauty and sensuality of the longing expressed in its phrases.

JUDITH ERNST
Chapel Hill, North Carolina
March 2002

Text Equivalents
in the King James Bible

For Further Reading

Ayo, Nicholas. *Sacred Marriage: The Wisdom of the Song of Songs.* New York: Continuum Publishing Group, 1997.

Bloch, Channa & Ariel. *The Song of Songs: A New Translation with an Introduction and Commentary.* New York: Random House, 1995.

Exum, Cheryl. *Song of Songs: A Commentary.* Old Testament Library. London: SCM; Louisville, KY: Westminster John Knox Press, forthcoming.

Falk, Marcia. *The Song of Songs: A New Translation and Interpretation.* San Francisco: HarperCollins, 1990.

Fox, Michael V. *The Song of Songs and the Ancient Egyptian Love Songs.* Madison: University of Wisconsin Press, 1985.

Guyon, Jeanne Marie. *Song of Songs.* New Kensington, PA: Whitaker House, 1997.

Keel, Othmar. *The Song of Songs: A Continental Commentary.* Minneapolis: Fortress Press, 1994.

Longman, Tremper. *Song of Songs*. Grand Rapids: Wm. B. Eerdmans Publishing Co., 2001.

Murphy, Roland Edmund. *The Song of Songs: A Commentary on the Book of Canticles or the Song of Songs*. Minneapolis: Augsburg Publishing House, 1994.

Zohary, Michael. *Plants of the Bible*. London: Cambridge University Press, 1982.

DATE DUE